Louise Otzen
Sophia Rasmussen

Destination

England

Cornelsen

 http://www.cornelsen.de

1. Auflage, 2. Druck 2010

© 2005 Cornelsen Verlag, Berlin
© Original edition, Copyright Copenhagen 2004 by Gyldendalske Boghandel, Nordisk Forlag A/S

Druck: Narayana Press, Dänemark

ISBN 978-3-06-031226-9

Fotos

Umschlag: www.britainonview.com

S.1 o: www.britainonview.com, **S. 1 u:** www.britainonview.com, **S. 6:** www.britainonview.com,
S. 7: www.britainonview.com, **S. 8 o:** www.britainonview.com, **S. 8 u:** www.britainonview.com,
S. 9 o: Den Britiske Ambassade, **S. 9 u:** The Oxford Illustrated History of the British Monarchy, Oxford University
Press, **S. 10:** www.britainonview.com, **S. 11:** www.britainonview.com, **S. 12 o:** www.britainonview.com,
S. 12 u: Britiske Billeder, Gyldendal, **S. 13:** www.britainonview.com, **S. 14:** www.britainonview.com,
S. 14/15: www.britainonview.com, **S. 15:** www.britainonview.com, **S. 16:** www.britainonview.com,
S. 16/17: www.britainonview.com, **S. 17:** www.britainonview.com, **S. 18:** www.britainonview.com,
S. 19 o: Gyldendals Billedbibliotek, **S. 19 u:** The Bayeux Tapestry, **S. 20:** www.britainonview.com,
S. 20/21: www.britainonview.com, **S. 21:** www.britainonview.com, **S. 22:** 150 Years of Photo Journalism, Viol. I,
Könemann, **S. 23:** Gyldendals Billedbibliotek, **S. 25:** Gyldendals Billedbibliotek, **S. 26:** Poul Lakatos/Polfoto,
S. 27 o: Gyldendals Billedbibliotek, **S. 27 u:** Britiske Billeder, Gyldendal, **S. 28:** Gyldendals Billedbibliotek,
S. 29: Britiske Billeder, Gyldendal, **S. 30:** www.britainonview.com, **S. 31:** Adam Woolfitt/Corbis,
S. 32: Polfoto, **S. 33:** www.britainonview.com/Howard Saver, **S. 34:** Scanpix Danmark, **S. 35:** www.britainonview.com,
S. 36: www.britainonview.com, **S. 37 u:** www.britainonview.com, **S. 37 o:** Graham Tim/Corbis Sygma,
S. 38: www.britainonview.com, **S. 39:** Corbis, **S. 40:** www.britainonview.com, **S. 41:** www.britainonview.com,
S. 42: www.britainonview.com, **S. 43:** Kim Agersten/Polfoto, **S. 44:** www.britainonview.com,
S. 45: www.britainonview.com, **S. 46/47:** www.britainonview.com, **S. 48 o:** Hulton-Deutsch Collection/Corbis,
S. 48 u: www.britainonview.com, **S. 49:** Photo B.D.V./Corbis, **S. 50:** www.britainonview.com,
S. 50/51: www.britainonview.com, **S. 51:** www.britainonview.com, **S. 52:** www.britainonview.com,
S. 53: www.britainonview.com, **S. 54 o:** www.britainonview.com, **S. 54 u:** www.britainonview.com,
S. 55: www.britainonview.com, **S. 56:** www.britainonview.com, **S. 57:** Darren Starling/Polfoto,
S. 58: www.britainonview.com, **S. 59:** www.britainonview.com.

Contents

England – A First Glance   6

National Symbols   8

Geography   10

London   14

England Under Attack   18

Two Great Rulers: Henry VIII and Elizabeth I   20

The Industrial Revolution   22

From Empire to Commonwealth   24

The World Wars   27

The British Parliament   30

The Monarchy   33

Religion   35

The English   38

Schools   42

Working England   46

Sport and Competition   50

English Traditions   54

English Food   57

Vocabulary   60

Glasgow ■

Ed

SCOTLA

North Channel

**NORTHERN
IRELAND**

● **Belfast**

Isle of
Man

● Douglas

*I R I S H
S E A*

Black

Live

Dublin ●

Holyhead ●

Caernarfon
Bay

▲
Snowdon

IRELAND

Cardigan
Bay

WALE

Aberystwyth ●

● Cardigan

ST GEORGE'S CHANNEL

Swansea
●

Cardi

Bristol Ch

Lundy
Island

●
Ilfracombe

Bude ●

Exeter ●

Dartmoor

Plymouth ●

Land's
End   ● Penzance

Lyme Bay

*Isles of
Scilly*

Lizard Point

Facts and Statistics

Area: 130,439 square kilometres

Population: 49,753,000

Capital city: London

Currency: £ = Pounds, p = pence

Dominant religion: Christianity

Piccadilly Circus in London.

England –
A First Glance

A visit to England gives you many different impressions; from the noise and colour of London's busy streets to the peaceful rolling hills in central England, or from the bag-lady to the business man in his pin-striped suit or maybe it's the queuing for the bus or the fish and chips shop.

People are often confused by the many different names: The British Isles, England, Great Britain, The United Kingdom. What is what?

The British Isles refers to the two large islands – and the hundreds of small islands surrounding them – that are found off the northwest coast of Europe. The largest island, and the one closest to Europe, is called Great Britain. This island includes England, Scotland and Wales. The smaller island is Ireland. Most of Ireland is an independent state, which is officially called the Republic of Ireland. Its Irish name is Eire, but usually people call it Ireland or sometimes just the Republic. The northeastern part of the island is called Northern Ireland. Despite its name, the area is not an individual state. It is under the authority of the British government in London.

The official name for all of the British areas (i.e. Scotland, Wales, England and Northern Ireland) is the United Kingdom of Great Britain and Northern Ireland. As this is quite a mouthful, most people say the United Kingdom, or they shorten it to the UK. Many simply call it Britain, and the word the British is used about things or people from the UK.

This book focuses on England and will deal with what is characteristic about England.

Landscape from the Lake District.

National Symbols

The Union Jack.

When the first version of the union flag was created in 1606, it only consisted of the cross of St George and the cross of St Andrew. It was not until 1801 that the cross of St Patrick was included in the last and final version of the flag. Wales has never been represented in the Union Jack, because Wales was already united with England in 1606, so one did not need to illustrate Wales as a separate country. Wales has its own flag. It is a red dragon standing on a green field under a white sky, and this flag is even older than the Union Jack. The Welsh flag was created during the 15th century, and it is still used regularly.

The Welsh flag.

When you are in England, the flag that you see most often is the British flag. This flag is called the Union Flag, or more often the Union Jack. The name comes from the fact that it is a combination of three separate flags. The English flag is a red cross on a white background. The red cross is the sign that was given to St George, the patron saint of England. The Scottish flag is the white diagonal cross of St Andrew, the patron saint of Scotland, on a blue background. Finally, there is the diagonal red cross on a white background that represents Ireland and the Irish patron saint, St Patrick.

The Royal Coat of Arms.

The Royal Coat of Arms

The three nations that make up the United Kingdom are also represented in the Royal Coat of Arms. The shield in the centre shows the nation's symbols. The three lions of England can be seen in the top left and bottom right corners, the lion of Scotland is in the top right corner, and in the last corner there is the harp of Ireland. The shield is supported by the English lion and the Scottish unicorn, and it rests upon green grass in which one can see the red rose for England, the thistle for Scotland and the green shamrock for Ireland.

Saint George – The Patron Saint of England

The most famous legend about St George is his meeting with a dragon. In this story, a village in Libya was being terrorised by a dragon. The locals gave it lots of sheep hoping that after it had enough to eat, it would go away. Sadly, the sheep did not satisfy the dragon, and the villagers started offering people to the hungry dragon instead. Then, just as the local princess was to be sacrificed, George came along. He killed the dragon and rescued the princess. The dragon is often seen as a symbol of Satan, and the princess represents Christianity. Nobody knows if the legend is true or not, but George was made a saint because of his reputation as a defender of Christianity.

freaky facts:

Why are English stamps the only stamps in the world that do not have their country name written on them? England was the first country to use stamps, so it was not necessary to write where the stamps came from. People automatically recognised them.

St George killing the dragon.

Geography

The Peak District.

Facts and Statistics

Highest mountain: Scafell Pike in the Lake District, 978 m

Longest river: the Severn, 354 km

Largest lake: Windermere in the Lake District, 17 km long

Major cities: London, Birmingham, Liverpool, Manchester

Land marks: White Cliffs of Dover, Lands End, Cheddar Gorge, Stonehenge

England stretches from the southern tip of Cornwall, Lizard Point, to the most northern town, Berwick-upon-Tweed on the border to Scotland. The country is known as 'the green and pleasant land', and it has many different types of landscape.

About two hours drive north from London, travellers will see the first hills of The Peak District at the southern end of the Pennines. The Pennines is a long range of mountains, which is often called the backbone of Britain.

Further north and towards the west coast there is one of England's famous walking areas: The Lake District. This area has more visitors every year than any other region in the entire British Isles. It is home to some of England's most beautiful scenery including the country's highest mountain and longest lake. The scenery has inspired many of England's poets and artists.

The eastern and southern regions are mostly low-lands, which are used for farming. A characteristic feature of the English countryside is the trees, hedges and stone walls that surround many fields. These are a great help to wildlife as they give birds and animals places to live. In the past hundred years, many farmers have pulled out the hedges to create even larger fields and earn more money.

The English weather changes so often that there is always something to say about it. Even though England is quite far north, the climate is mild, and the country seldom has extreme conditions. This is because the warm Gulf Stream from the Atlantic Ocean flows down the west coast and heats the air. All year round the temperatures are slightly higher in the western parts of England, but these areas also get more snow and rain than the rest of the country. Summer temperatures in southern

Fields surrounded by stone walls.

Cloudy weather.

less and less, as England's European neighbours started to produce their own coal. This meant that many coal mines had to close, leading to massive unemployment and the death of many towns.

Jobs in the north have often paid less than jobs anywhere else in England. People from the north get cancer and suffer from heart problems more often than southerners. Schools in the north have poorer exam results and greater problems with pupils that stay away from school, than they do in the southern areas. As a result, many people have moved to the south.

Miners in Kent at the beginning of the 20th century.

England are between 23-25°C, but it is unusual for any area to have a dry period of more than two to three weeks. During the winter the eastern regions are usually the coldest and wettest.

The North-South Divide

Earning a living in the north has not always been easy, but for a short period of time the north was very rich. At the end of the 18th century, large amounts of coal and iron were found in the Pennines. Iron became important in the production of all kinds of machines, and the coal provided the power that was needed to keep the machines working. For the next 200 years, the north contributed to the growth in England's economy. England was able to extract so much coal from the ground that it started exporting it to other countries. During the 20th century, the mines exported

A village in the heart of England; Bourton-on-the-Water.

Southern England, with its good farming land and close to London, has always attracted a lot of people and been relatively rich. Already during the 17th century, 10% of the population lived in London, and this trend still continues today.

The migration from the north has caused problems for London and the southern regions. As the population of London has expanded, life has become stressful. Motorists experience daily traffic jams and often find it difficult to find parking spaces. Even the underground system has begun to suffer. Not enough money has been spent on repairing and developing the systems and now tubes are often delayed. To get away from the constant bustle of city life, many people buy houses in smaller towns or villages. They keep their city jobs, and commute to work, either by car or train. But, as more and more people want to move away from London, it has become difficult to find houses in the surrounding areas, and the search for a house moves even further away. Nowadays, many commuters are willing to live 200-250 km away from London, and they typically spend up to four hours travelling to work and back every day!

The small towns and villages have also changed. They used to have a variety of small shops, but as the commuters spend very little time in the villages, there is hardly any business during the week. As a result, many shops have had to close, and 30% of England's villages do not even have a pub! Instead many large shopping centres with big supermarkets are being built on the outskirts of the middle-sized towns.

London

London is the centre of all political and economic life in England. It covers 300 km² and with a population of 7 million people it is the largest city in Europe.

One of the most famous buildings is the Houses of Parliament, which is also called the Palace of Westminster. This is where England is governed from. The Palace is built by the River Thames and is 280 metres long with 3 km of passages. It has 11 court-yards, 100 staircases and over 1,000 rooms. At the north end stands the impressive clock tower from 1858, better known as Big Ben. Big Ben is the largest bell in the tower. It weighs 13.8 tonnes and it was named after its maker, a large Welshman called Sir Benjamin Hall. The tower is 96.3 metres tall, and each clock face has a diameter of 7 metres.

A few minutes away from Parliament is the Queen's London home, Buckingham Palace. The Royal Family bought the Palace in 1762, but nobody was happy living there. Later, Queen Victoria complained that the rooms were cold and dirty, and that the fireplaces smoked too much. Since her reign, a lot of money has been spent on improving the Palace, both inside and outside. Many Londoners think that the building is ugly, but they still like to visit the Palace to see the royal ceremonies like the Changing of the Guard.

Big Ben.

Buckingham Palace.

The Tower of London is one of the finest medieval fortresses in Europe. It dates back to the 11th century. Originally, it was a fortress to protect London from enemies. Later, it was used as a palace for the Royal Family, and for a period it became the prison that housed some of England's most famous prisoners like Henry VI and Richard II. The Princes Edward and Richard, who were only boys at the time, were murdered in one of the towers, which is now known as the 'Bloody Tower'. Two of Henry VIII's wives were also imprisoned and lost their lives under the executioner's axe. Executions did not always go as planned. It took five swings of the axe and some cutting before the Earl of Monmouth's head fell off!

Fortunately, a visit to the Tower is no longer a frightening experience. The fortress is now a museum. One of the main attractions is the Crown Jewels. The Imperial State Crown contains 2,800 diamonds and the Royal Sceptre holds one of the largest diamonds in the world, the Star of Africa. The Tower is guarded by the traditional Beefeaters in their colourful uniforms that date back to 1552.

A Beefeater at the Tower of London.

freaky
facts:

London used to be renowned for being foggy all year round. This was because the city's houses all had coal heaters that produced thousands of tiny particles of soot that spread over the roofs and gave the foggy appearance. Now that cleaner forms of central heating have been introduced, London is no longer covered in sooty fog.

St Paul's Cathedral.

freaky facts:

Why is the population of London three times bigger than that of Athens, but covers an area of land that is ten times larger?
The English like their privacy, and they have never really liked living in flats. Everybody wants his or her own house. As a result, English cities usually spread outwards instead of upwards.

The most important church in London is St Paul's Cathedral, which is the largest cathedral in England. It has been used for major events such as the burial of Winston Churchill and the wedding of Prince Charles and Lady Diana. From the outside the cathedral looks like St Peter's in Rome because of its massive dome. A special feature in the cathedral is the Whispering Gallery at the base of the dome. This is famous because of its unusual acoustics. If one whispers a message to the stone wall, it will be heard on the other side of the dome 33 metres away!

Madame Tussaud's is one of the most popular exhibitions in England with over 2.7 million visitors a year. It is filled with wax figures of famous people from all over the world. The museum is divided into seven sections ranging from Superstars and the Chamber of Horrors to Royalty and Sport's Stars. The French woman Marie Tussaud founded the museum in 1802. Before moving to England, she made death masks of some of the victims of the French Revolution.

An interesting place to shop is the department store Harrods. In 1849, Harrods was just a small grocery store with two assistants. Now, it is a super store with 300 departments selling everything from pets to paper clips. The food department is in the centre of the building, and here it is possible to buy 150 different types of bread, 300 different kinds of cheese and, because it is England, 151 different varieties of tea. 35,000 customers come to visit the store every day. At night, the outside of the store is lit up with 11,500 light bulbs.

Harrods at night.

The London Eye.

These are a handful of the traditional sights that are on the 'must' list for London. The newest attraction, which was built to celebrate the year 2000, is the giant wheel 'the London Eye'. This wheel will give you a bird's eye view of the City of London.

Hadrian's Wall in northern England was built by the Romans.

England Under Attack

During its early history, England was attacked by four different invading forces. The first to come were the Romans, who arrived in England around 43 AD and occupied the country for nearly 400 years. The Romans forced their way of life upon the local population (the Celts), but when they left, the country could thank them for a system of straight stone roads, which were needed to transport the Roman troops between the major outposts. Their language, Latin, was spoken by the elite and by the church. Many English words originate from Latin. For example the word 'exit' comes from 'to go out' in Latin.

When the Romans left, England was overrun by Angles and Saxons from Northern Europe. These Anglo Saxons quickly controlled the south east of the island while the legendary King Arthur and his Knights of the Round Table controlled the west. Legend says that King Arthur won his kingdom by pulling his sword, Excalibur, from a huge stone. This sword was thrown into a big lake when Arthur died.

From 499 the Vikings often ruined the peace in England. These warriors were tempted by Britain's wealth. Sailing over the North Sea from Denmark and Norway, they raided the east coast of England. They burnt the monasteries and stole the church silver and returned home. Later in 865, the Vikings conquered the north and east of England and settled there until they were challenged by the Saxon King Alfred the Great. He made a peace agreement with the Vikings dividing England between them. 'Danelaw' made up the north and east, while

Canute (Knud) the Great.

Alfred controlled 'Wessex', the south and west of the country. The Vikings stayed for over 150 years and in 1016, led by Canute (Knud) the Great, they took over England completely. One of the taxes during that time was called 'Danegeld', meaning Danish money, which was paid to the Danish warriors. In 1028, Canute was made King of England, and he ruled for 17 years. After his death the Vikings lost their influence in England.

In 1066, England was attacked and conquered for the last time. This was the year that Duke William from Normandy defeated the English forces at the Battle of Hastings. After the battle, William was crowned King of England in Westminster Abbey. He rewarded his soldiers by giving them English land.

All the people living on that land became their slaves, and the feudal system began. This meant that the King had total control of the country. Next came the great noblemen, who later became the aristocracy of England. Then there were noblemen, who only owned a village or two. Finally came the peasants who had no rights at all and were controlled by their masters. They could not even marry or travel without their masters' permission. The noblemen spoke French, and the priests and monks used Latin. The peasants were the only people who spoke English, and it was a long time before English was spoken by everybody. The Norman period ended in 1135 when William's son died, and another branch of the family took over the throne.

freaky facts:

Alfred the Great travelled around England in disguise organising resistance against the Vikings. Once, while staying with a peasant woman, he was asked to watch some cakes cooking, so they would not burn. The King was so deep in thought that he let the cakes burn. The story goes that the woman was very angry and accused him of being lazy. Alfred only laughed at the idea of the King being told off.

Scenes from the Battle of Hastings in the Bayeux Tapestry.

Two Great Rulers:
Henry VIII and Elizabeth I

King Henry VIII.

The Tudor family ruled England from 1485 to 1603. This was a time for great change and development for the country. The first Tudor king, Henry VII, united England after many years of war and made England rich again. When he died in 1509 the throne was passed on to Henry VIII. The young King Henry did a lot to stimulate culture and education and some of England's great centres of learning were founded at this time. Henry is also well known for his six wives. Two he had beheaded, one died, two he put under house arrest and one was alive when he died himself. (Read more about Henry VIII and his wives on p. 36)

freaky facts:

'Off with his head'. During the Tudor period, it was not safe to be an important person. More than half of all the important people of this period were executed. Very few people who walked into the Tower of London by Traitors' Gate were seen again – alive!

Traitors' Gate at the Tower of London.

Henry VIII was followed by his daughter, Elizabeth, in 1558. Even though she was a young girl when she came to the throne, she ruled for many years and was known as the Virgin Queen, because she never married. It was during Elizabeth's reign that the Spanish tried to attack England to make the population become Catholics. In 1588, the Spanish Armada sailed up the English Channel. The Armada was a fleet of enormous galleons, which should have had no trouble beating the English navy. Fortunately, with the help of bad weather and their smaller ships the English won the battle.

Queen Elizabeth 1.

freaky
facts:

'God bless you' is said when somebody sneezes. This saying dates back to the time of the great plague in 1348. Sneezing was one of the last symptoms before death, and people wanted God to bless the victims before they died.

ROOM, LANCASHIRE COTTON MILL. 62174. J.V.

The Industrial Revolution

At about the same time as the revolutions in America and France, there was another revolution whose effect on people was even more extensive. This revolution started in England in 1775 and was called the Industrial Revolution. The word industry originally meant hard manual work, but with the Industrial Revolution this hard work was taken over by machines. Machines were not new and were already used, but with new knowledge steam was introduced, and this made the machines much more powerful and efficient. There were machines that could be used for the production of coal and minerals and the manufacture of many kinds of goods such as textiles. There were also machines to help in the fields and an agricultural revolution went hand in hand with the industrial one. Trains and steamships helped to transport the goods around both the country and the world.

The Industrial Revolution meant that many people moved from the country to the towns looking for work in the new industries. The factory owners employed many children and women. There were three main reasons for this. Firstly, their labour was cheap. Secondly, the children could easily crawl under the machines to repair them and to keep them clean. And thirdly, children could be ordered around by the foremen. Conditions for children working in the coalmines were even worse. In 1842, the Mines Report was published. This said that children under five worked underground for 12 hours a day for just two pennies. Children often stood in water up to their thighs and were whipped if they worked slowly.

This report shocked England and led to new laws that protected the workers, and from then on conditions gradually improved. Education became compulsory and free, and many hospitals were built. One of the important people of this time was the nurse, Florence Nightingale, who worked to improve the quality of nursing in hospitals. Just by introducing basic rules of hygiene, such as clean sheets and washing hands, she was able to reduce the death rate amongst the patients dramatically.

Florence Nightingale.

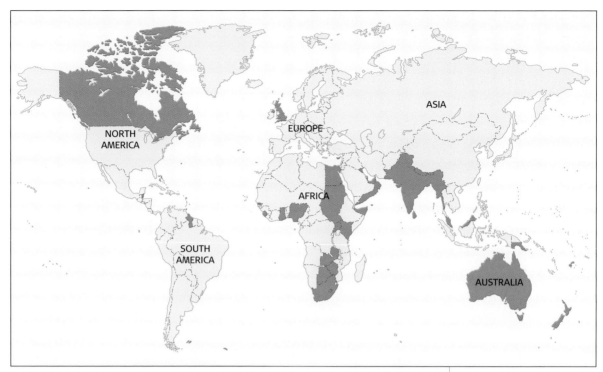

The British Empire.

From Empire to Commonwealth

The roots of the British Empire started in the 1500s when Queen Elizabeth I encouraged exploration of the New World. Many adventurers went to sea to look for new lands and exotic treasures. At this time, there were already trading companies in Turkey, Russia and the East Indies, but the Queen expected the explorers to settle in the newly discovered lands and create colonies.

In 1607, Sir Walter Raleigh brought back tobacco from America, and a colony was started there and named 'Virginia' after the Virgin Queen, Elizabeth. In 1620, a small group of Puritans set sail in the Mayflower and started the colony of New Plymouth. By the end of 17th century England had founded 13 colonies in North America.

Throughout the 18th century, many European countries fought to gain power in the New World. In 1763, a treaty was signed in France allowing Britain to keep all her colonies, and this made her the leading world power. English was being spoken in many different parts of the world, and by the end of the 19th century Britain controlled most of the oceans and 20% of the land areas of the world and 23% of the population. The Empire stretched from Great Britain in the north to South Africa in the south and from Canada in the west to Australia and New Zealand in the east. It was said that the sun never set on the British Empire.

Sir Walter Raleigh.

Two of the more important colonies were India and Australia. Unusual spices like pepper and nutmeg, textiles like silk and cotton, indigo and sugar were among the specialities that could be bought from India. It was these items that encouraged the English to trade with the country. The colonisation of India was not planned because of this trade, but was the result of an impulsive action by a man called Robert Clive in the East India Company. In 1750, Clive heard of an incident in Calcutta where some British citizens were captured and put in prison in a tiny hole where they all died of suffocation. This place was later known as the Black Hole of Calcutta. He was so angry about this that he gathered a group of soldiers and seized the province of Bengal for the East Indian Company. The rest of the conquest of India was not so quick as it took over 150 years to take over the remaining states. India became known as the Jewel in the Crown of the Empire.

Australia was a different story. Although Australian pre-history goes back 47,000 years it was not until 1606 that the Dutch found Australia and called it New Holland. This was not to last, for just over a hundred years later, Captain James Cook sailed from England and took possession of the eastern half of Australia. The English began to settle there around 1788 and soon after that it became a place where England transported its criminals to. All sorts of people were sent for all sorts of crimes. The people could be orphans, aristocrats, women or pickpockets, and the crimes could range from theft, receiving stolen goods, stealing fish from a pond or river, stealing plants and trees or illegally marrying someone. It was not until 1844 that this practice was stopped, and Australia became a free land for everyone.

Hong Kong was under British rule from 1860 to 1997, when it was returned to China. England had used Hong Kong as a trading post from the 18th century. Tea, silk and illegal opium were the important goods. The Chinese felt that the British were becoming too powerful and tried to throw them out of China. This resulted in two 'Opium Wars' in 1841 and 1860. The British won these wars and took possession of Hong Kong. In 1898 China and Great Britain signed an agreement which allowed Great Britain to rent Hong Kong for the next 99 years.

From the middle of the 19th century the idea of democracy began to spread to colonies such as Canada, New Zealand and Australia. These countries wanted to become independent states, but at the same time they did not want to lose their close connection to England. As a result the Commonwealth of Nations was formed in 1931. The Commonwealth gave the former colonies the possibility to co-operate and trade with each other.

After the Second World War, more and more of the colonies gained independence. India in 1947, and the first African colony to become an independent country was Ghana in 1957. During the next 40 years, the rest of the colonies became independent, and most of them became members of the Commonwealth of Nations. South Africa left the Commonwealth in 1961 because of its Apartheid policy, and returned in 1994 after the country had held its first democratic election. Nigeria was suspended from 1995 to 1999, because the country continued to ignore human rights. Today there are 54 member countries.

Commonwealth Day is celebrated every year on the second Monday in March, and the Commonwealth Games, which is a sports competition, is held every four years in one of the member countries.

The ceremony that marked Hong Kong's return to China.

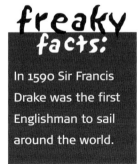

freaky facts:

In 1590 Sir Francis Drake was the first Englishman to sail around the world.

The World Wars

Campaign poster from the First World War.

There were about 40,000 kilometres of trenches. Put end to end they would reach all the way round the earth. The soldiers lived and fought from these trenches in the most terrible conditions. The trenches were 2 to 2½ metres deep and were built up with sand bags on the enemy's side. They were cold, wet, filled with rats and smelled of rum, dirt and dead bodies. Many new technologies were also used like explosive mines, tanks, machine guns and poison gas, and by 1917 both sides had bomber planes. The casualties in this war were terrible.

A trench in the First World War.

The First World War

The First World War is also called the Great War. It lasted from 1914–1918 and was supposed to be 'the War to End All Wars'. The British government started a propaganda campaign to encourage men to join the army. The campaign appealed to men's sense of duty. Posters with slogans like 'Your Country Needs YOU', 'Daddy, What Did YOU Do In The Great War?' and 'The Women of Britain Say Go' were seen all over the country. In the beginning many men volunteered. They believed that they were going to fight a heroic battle for freedom and democracy. But the reality was the trenches.

From July to November 1916, the British lost 400,000 men, and the total death toll for Britain was 750,000 men. Over 8.5 million people were killed on all sides during the First World War. The soldiers that survived the war returned home traumatised by what they had been through. Many of them suffered from shell shock, which often ended in a complete mental breakdown.

One of the very few positive aspects of the war was the improvement of women's situation in British society. This began with women taking men's jobs in factories. By 1918, women over the age of 30 gained the right to vote. Ten years later, women were given the same right as men; everyone of 21 and over was allowed to vote.

freaky facts:

During the Second World War all street signs and sign posts were removed, so if the Germans were to land in Britain, they would have great difficulty in finding their way around, both in the countryside and in the towns.

The Second World War

After the First World War, peace treaties were signed. An uneasy calm settled over Europe. Sadly, the treaties did not work, and by the end of the 1930s the Second World War began.

In March 1939, Hitler's Germany attacked Czechoslovakia, and on September 1st, 1939, his army invaded Poland. All hopes of peace vanished and Britain, led by Winston Churchill, felt that it must enter the war to fight for democracy.

Winston Churchill.

The most important fight for Britain took place from 10th July 1940 until 31st October, 1940. This was known as the Battle of Britain. The Royal Air Force (RAF) only had 640 fighter planes to defend the country against 2,600 fighter and bomber planes from Germany.

The Battle of Britain was fought in four stages. In the first stage, the German Luftwaffe attacked coastal towns and convoys of ships in the English Channel. Their planes also flew over England to collect information about the British positions. In the second stage, the Germans started bombing British airfields. Their plan was to destroy the airforce on the ground and in the air. The third stage is known as 'the Blitz'. This was when the Germans carried out daytime bomb attacks against London and many other important targets. The British fighter pilots flew out to meet the German planes, before they could drop their bombs. As a result the Germans changed their tactics and attacked at night instead. In the fourth and last stage of the Battle of Britain, the RAF had developed night fighters and they were hitting more and more German planes. Towards the end of October the weather got worse, and there were fewer and fewer German raids. The German army realised that it would not be able to crush the British, so it decided to focus its forces on Russia.

60,000 people were killed in the bombing raids and London and many major towns were left in ruins, which took years to rebuild. By 1941 over 1.5 million people had joined volunteer groups in England to help in any way they could by working in factories, on farms and in hospitals.

Bombed-out London, October 1940.

The Second World War was a total war. No one was safe; it was accepted to kill children, women and old people while attacking civilian targets. In England, children were sent to the country to keep them safe, and those remaining in towns spent much of their time in air raid shelters. Food was in short supply and much of it was rationed. There were no more bananas, chocolate or ice cream to be found. Not only food was rationed but also petrol, furniture and clothes.

The war ended in 1945 when Berlin was surrounded by allied troops. Hitler committed suicide on 30th April, 1945, and with his death the war gradually came to an end.

The British Parliament

The Houses of Parliament.

The United Kingdom is a democracy that is run by a parliament. Parliament is the highest authority, and it is responsible for making the laws of the country. The British Parliament consists of three parts:

- The House of Commons
- The House of Lords
- The Crown

The House of Commons has 659 members or 'MPs' as they are called (Members of Parliament), who are elected by the people in general elections. Anyone over the age of 21 can become a candidate, if he or she can pay a deposit of £500. The money is given back if the person wins more than 5% of the votes in their constituency. Only very few people take a chance as an independent candidate, as most candidates belong to a political party.

Government is formed after a general election by the party which has won the most votes. If the Government wishes to make changes in the way the country is run, it must introduce its ideas in Parliament. Both Houses of Parliament discuss the issues, and if a law needs to be made or changed all three parts of Parliament have to agree.

The House of Lords is not a democratic institution like the House of Commons. Unlike the MPs, the Lords are unpaid, and they are not elected by the people. The number of members is not fixed. In 2002 there were 700 members. They include 26 bishops and archbishops, 9 senior judges, 92 hereditary peers (people from the aristocracy that have inherited their place in the House of Lords) and the rest are 'life peers' (people who will be members for the rest of their lives). The position of life peer was introduced in 1958 to honour people that have done excellent work for the country.

The Crown, which is the third part in Parliament, refers to the Queen. She is the Head of State and a symbol of the unity of the country. The Queen does not take part in the political discussions herself, but she has weekly meetings with the Prime Minister, who tells her about what is going on in Parliament. She is free to decide herself, but it is tradition that the Crown follows the advice of the Government.

The system of political parties has existed since the 18th century, and for a long time there has been a two-party system. Since 1945, the competition for power has been between the Conservative and the Labour Party. The Conservative Party, whose members are nicknamed the 'Tories', believes in economic freedom, law and order and patriotism. Traditionally, the party has won votes from people who are wealthy and who do not support the European Union, while the Labour Party focuses more on the well-being of society as a whole than on the rights of the individual. There are also a number of smaller parties represented in the House of Commons like the Liberal Democrats and the Scottish Nationalists.

The shape of the debating room in the House of Commons is very special, because it is designed to fit the two-party system. The room is rectangular, and the Speaker's Chair is at one end. On either side of the room there are long benches, and it is tradition that the Government sits on the right hand side of the Chair. On the left hand side sits the largest minority party, which is called the Opposition. The leaders of the Government and the Opposition sit on the front benches. The other MPs sit behind them and are called the 'backbenchers'.

The Debating Room in the House of Commons.

freaky facts:

The word parliament comes from the French 'parler'- to talk.

freaky facts:

After each election the MPs elect 'the Speaker'. The Speaker acts as chairman in all political debates. The Speaker makes sure that all opinions are heard in a discussion. It is also the Speaker's job to make sure that the rules of the House are followed. It is expected that all members take part actively in the debates. For this reason MPs are neither allowed to eat, drink nor read newspapers and magazines during the discussions. MPs are not allowed to read prepared speeches either, as this can make the discussions long and boring. Usually the debates are both lively and noisy, as MPs often interrupt each other. The Speaker can stop a discussion if he or she feels that MPs are rude to each other. Some of the words the Speakers have objected to through the years have been coward, hooligan, rat, swine and traitor. MPs are not allowed to call each other liars, and they are banished from Parliament if they do.

Former Prime Minister Tony Blair during a debate.

The Queen and Prince Philip in the State Coach.

The Monarchy

England has been a monarchy since the ninth century. At that time, the king or queen was the supreme head of the country and ruled over the church and the people. Over the centuries, as democracy began to develop, the monarchy gradually lost its power. In the 1860s and 1870s, the government discussed removing the Royal Family and making Britain into a republic. Queen Victoria was queen at that time and she worked together with the Prime Minister to change the role of the monarchy. Victoria created new ceremonies so that the people could see the Royal Family more often. She also tried to show the population that the Royal Family was a family like other families and soon the public began to support the monarchy again.

Today the monarch acts as a symbolic leader of the United Kingdom, and many people associate the Monarchy with two things. Firstly, the many colourful ceremonies like the State Opening of Parliament, when the Queen travels by a horse-drawn carriage from Buckingham Palace to the Houses of Parliament. Secondly, the scandals that hit the Royal Family during the 1990s. It was felt that too much of the tax-payers' money was being spent on luxuries, such as the royal train and the royal yacht, which together cost £11.5 million per year. Then came the divorces that covered the front pages of all the newspapers and magazines. One of these was the break-up of Prince Charles and Princess Diana's marriage. Princess Diana was extremely popular all over the world, amongst other things because of her charitable work. The nation and the world were shocked by her tragic death in August 1997, and the whole country showed their admiration and love by following her funeral. Since then the Royal Family has tried to modernize itself to regain the respect and a place in the heart of the population.

freaky facts:

It is well known that on several occasions clever conmen have tried to sell the Queen's home Buckingham Palace to naive American tourists.

Prince Charles and Princess Diana.

Stonehenge.

Religion

- There are 7.9 million active members of various religions (both Christian and non-Christian) in the UK
- **The Anglican Church** is responsible for 42 cathedrals and 16,000 other church buildings
- **The Methodist Church** is the largest of the Free Churches with 353,000 believers
- There are between 1,5 and 2 million **Muslims** in the UK
- The first **Sikh temple** (called a gurd-wara) was built in London in 1911
- On 22nd June every year, modern **druids** meet at Stonehenge to cele-brate the summer solstice

[Foreign and Commonwealth Office, 2001]

Druids

Religious activity goes back many thousands of years. The impressive and famous Stonehenge, built on the Salisbury Plain sometime between 2500–1500 BC, was used by the druids for religious ceremonies. At that time, people believed that there were many Gods to whom they prayed. Amongst other things they worshipped fire and water. The druids were priests, and for feast days they gathered mistletoe from oak trees to give to the people, who thought it would protect them from illness and unhappiness. The druids also sacri-ficed white cows to please the Gods.

Canterbury Cathedral.

The Christian Churches

In 2000, about 40 million citizens thought of themselves as Christians. Only a small group of these people are 'active believers', who go to church on a regular basis. There are many different types of Christian churches and communities, but one has a special status in England. This is the Anglican Church of England.

England used to be a Catholic country, and the head of the Church was the Pope in Rome, but this changed under the rule of King Henry VIII in 1533. Henry was a strong-willed king, who liked to have his own way. He wanted a divorce from his wife, the Spanish Catholic, Catherine of Aragon. At this time, no one could get a divorce without permission from the Pope in Rome. Henry applied for permission, and it was refused, but he was still determined to divorce and to marry again, because he wanted a male heir to the throne. So he took the law into his own hands and broke away from the Church of Rome. Henry named himself Head of the Church of England and Defender of the Faith, and with one blow England became Protestant.

It is important to remember that Henry was not a religious reformer like Martin Luther, who also broke away from the Catholic Church. Henry's break with the Pope did not happen because he disliked the Catholic faith. He simply wanted his own way. At this point Henry, who was fond of money, became much richer, because he took over all that belonged to the church; its land, buildings and treasures. This time has come to be known as the English Reformation.

Since the reign of Henry VIII, British monarchs have had the title of 'Supreme Governor' of the Church of England. This gives them the power to appoint the archbishops, bishops and deans of the Church, though they usually follow the advice of the Church and the Prime Minister.

There are a number of different 'Free Churches' in England. 'Free Church' refers to a Protestant Church that is not the State Church (the Anglican Church). These include the Methodist, Baptist, Salvation Army and Pentecostal Churches.

The Shree Swaminarayan Mandir Temple in Neasden.

Other religions

The largest of the non-Christian religions is Islam. Muslims first started coming to Britain at the beginning of the 19th century. They were seamen and traders from the Middle East, Pakistan and Bangladesh and settled down in the large ports. However, the majority of the Muslims living in the UK came in the 1950s and 1960s when there were a lot of jobs.

The Central London Mosque at Regents Park.

Today, there are about 2 million Muslims. Many live in London, but there are also large Muslim communities in Liverpool, Manchester, Leicester, Birmingham and Bradford. There are over 1,000 mosques in the country, and approximately 900,000 Muslims are regular visitors in these mosques.

The Sikh and the Hindu communities are about the same size, each with approximately 500,000 members. The Sikhs have over 200 temples to worship in, while the Hindus only have 120.

The Jewish community is the oldest and one of the smallest religious communities. Jews already started settling in England during the Norman Conquest in 1066, but in 1290 King Edward I ordered all Jews to leave the country. They were not allowed back until 1651. The majority of the 300,000 Jews that live in England today were born and brought up in England, but their ancestors fled from persecution in Russia between 1881-1914 and from the Nazi regime during the Second World War.

The English

A policeman - a 'bobby'.

Many people have a fixed idea about who the English are. Some think of the bobby with his traditional helmet or of a Beefeater at the Tower of London. Others have an image of punks and hooligans. England has all these 'types' and many more. Some areas of the country have their own special identities, while other areas, especially the big cities are a mixture of people from different backgrounds and cultures.

Some of the people from the Northeast of England consider themselves to be Geordies. Apparently, the name comes from the time of King George III (1760-1820). It is thought that the people from the North who supported this unpopular king were called George's men or Geordies. Towards the end of his reign, George III was declared mad, and the word 'Geordie' then became a very negative word. This has long since changed and today, anyone born within one mile of the River Tyne, within the City of Newcastle upon Tyne, or anyone born between the River Tees and Tweed is proud to be called a Geordie.

Another area famous for its people is Liverpool. Its inhabitants are called Liverpudlians. They are well known for their razor sharp wit and humour and many have a career in music and show business. Take for example the Beatles.

A true Cockney is born within the sound of the bells of St Mary-le-Bow in the City of London. The Cockneys have a group of people known as the Pearly Kings and Queens. The name 'Pearly' comes from the countless pearl buttons that are sewn on to their clothes. The average number of pearl buttons used on one suit is 35,000. Cockney is also the name of the unique local accent, which is also known for its rhyming slang. Here are a few examples:

- *Wanna photo of me and the trouble and strife?* = Do you want a picture of me and my wife?
- *Move ya plates of meat up the apples and pears* = Move your feet up the stairs.
- *Use ya loaf of bread and put ya daisy roots on* = Use your head and put your boots on.

For a long time, England has been proud to be a multicultural society. 3,700,000 people are from ethnic minorities, half of whom are born in the UK. Over the past 200 years many immigrants have settled in England. Some of the first arrivals came in the 19th century. These were Jews, who had fled from oppression in Russia and Poland, Irish settlers escaping poverty, and then trade brought Indian and Chinese people to the main ports. In the 1930s,

freaky facts:

A well-known criminal from the Cockney area was Jack the Ripper. The Ripper murders took place in the slum area of Whitechapel. The Ripper killed 5 victims within five weeks in 1888. They were all Eastend prostitutes. The world's first serial killer was never caught.

Multicultural London.

'Gurning'.

refugees arrived from Nazi Germany and in the late 1940s West-Indians were encouraged to immigrate to England to help rebuild the country after the war. Since the 1950s, there have been waves of immigrants from Commonwealth nations, East Africa and Vietnam. More recently, there have been refugees from Rumania and the former Yugoslavia. This means that today nearly 200 languages are spoken across London. Famous immigrants include the psychologist Sigmund Freud, the philosopher Karl Marx and the footballer Mario Stanic.

Every day the identity of the English is changing because of the meeting of so many religions, cultures and nationalities. Very often this is reflected in the increasing number of festivals held around the country.

The oldest of the English festivals are often celebrated in the spring. Abbots Bromley Horn Dance takes place in Staffordshire. This dance is thought to be the oldest dance in Europe. It has been dated back to 1125 and may be even older. Six men carry reindeer antlers and perform dances and battles. These battles take place over a 32-km route around the village. The antlers that are used are over 900 years old.

In the Lake District there are some very unusual festivals such as 'Gurning' and 'The Biggest Liar'. Gurning is a competition to find out who can pull the funniest faces and the Biggest Liar is simply ... can you guess? In Gloucestershire people celebrate 'Whit Monday' with a 400-year-old custom of cheese rolling. A master of ceremonies rolls a round cheese down a very steep hill, and the local men try to catch it. In 1999, the race became so rough that one of the participants was seriously injured, and the festival was nearly stopped because of this.

Diwali is the Hindu festival of light. This festival lasts for two days, and on the second day, families let off fireworks and pray to keep evil spirits away. This is a new festival in England but ancient in India.

London's Notting Hill Carnival comes from the West Indies. The carnival was founded in 1966 as a small street festival. Since then it has become one of the largest street carnivals in the world with fantastic parades of beautiful costumes, elegant dancers and a wide variety of music – everything from reggae to rock.

Scene from the Notting Hill Carnival.

Schools

Facts and Statistics

- All children between the ages of 5 and 16 must go to school
- Approximately 70% of all young people choose to continue their education after they are 16
- 94% of pupils receive free education from the state, the remaining 6% go to private schools where parents pay for the school fees
- The average school class in primary school has 26 pupils

A schoolboy from Eton.

England has both free government-funded schools and private schools where parents pay the school fees. The first schools to be established were private. The famous boys' schools Winchester (1382) and Eton (1440) were started by monks to educate the children of the aristocracy. The golden age for private schools came at the end of the 19th century when many new schools were opened. These schools have played a large part in creating and spreading middle class values such as honesty, integrity and team spirit. At this time politicians realised that education should be available for everybody, and the local councils were encouraged to open schools for children between 5 and 13 years old. In 1944 a law was passed making free education obligatory for all children between 5 and 16, and this law is still followed today.

The school system:

Infant: 3-5 years old
Primary: 5-11 years old
Secondary: 11-16 years old
Six form colleges: 16 +

A normal school day starts at nine o'clock and finishes at three or four o'clock, sometimes later for the older pupils. At midday pupils have an hour's lunch break, and nearly 70% of all schools provide lunch for the pupils. School work is a mixture of class teaching and group work. In primary school, pupils only have one teacher who takes them for all subjects while in secondary schools pupils will have different teachers for most subjects.

School Uniforms

Uniforms were first given to poor school children in the 16th century and some of the first outfits looked like a monk's cassock. The richer children were allowed to dress as they wanted. In the 19th century most schools introduced uniforms for all pupils, and today all schools have them. There are many arguments for and against school uniforms. Most people say that uniforms save money, because parents do not have to spend a lot on designer labels, and pupils do not tease each other for wearing the 'wrong' brand of clothes. Some of the reasons against school uniforms are that all the children look alike, loose their individuality and they do not learn how to deal with people from different cultures and backgrounds.

Private or State School?

The majority of English children go to state schools while only 6% go to private schools. This is probably because the school fees are very expensive. During the last 10 years, the school fees have risen by 50%. Today, the average cost for a child at a private day school is £6,000 per year, and the cost of a year at boarding school is approximately double the amount.

What does one get for this money? Firstly a very good education and secondly social status. Traditionally, the schools with the best exam results are private schools. The private schools are extremely well equipped. They have all the facilities modern classrooms need, their sports grounds are professional, and they are able to employ some of the best teachers, simply because they can pay better

English schoolboys.

An overview of Oxford University.

wages. Parents who send their children to private schools want them to do well, and they take an active interest in their children's life at school. Former pupils from private schools fill a majority of the jobs in the ministries, the legal world, the army and the finance sector.

freaky
facts:

400,000 school children do not eat breakfast before they go to school.

Boarding Schools

Boarding schools have been a part of English society since the 14th century, and they were mainly used by the aristocracy and the rich. Today, only a small percent of pupils go to boarding schools, and the number is falling every year. Being at boarding school means that children from about the age of seven live at school, only seeing their parents at weekends, half terms and during the school holidays. The schools are usually organised into smaller units or houses to make the atmosphere as friendly and homely as possible. Lots of activities like drama, computer clubs and sport fill up the pupils' spare time.

Higher Education

The most famous universities in England are Oxford and Cambridge. They were founded in the 13th and 14th centuries. They have always attracted the best brains, and a degree from one of these universities opens many doors in life.

Oxford and Cambridge have many special traditions that affect everything from daily life to sport. Each college has a refectory (an eating hall), where both the students and teachers have their meals. The teachers and important guests sit at the 'high table', which is placed across the end of the hall. The students sit on benches at long tables. Nobody sits down or starts eating before somebody from the high table has said grace, which is a special prayer said before meals.

Sport plays a very important part of university life, and there are many competitions between the two universities. Traditionally, the Oxford teams wear dark blue and Cambridge light blue clothes. The media covers several of these sports, and the annual boat race (see p. 51 in Sport) and the rugby matches are followed by millions of fans.

In the 19th century, many new universities were opened to educate the growing number of students. These were nicknamed 'red-brick' universities, because they were built in modern style in contrast to the many beautiful and historic buildings of Oxford and Cambridge.

freaky facts:

An English school pupil's satchel weighs about 5.5 kilos.

King's College, Cambridge.

Working England

England is the 4th most important trading nation in the world. Some of the main areas are:

- **Aerospace**: Britain's aerospace industry is the biggest in Europe and handles every step in production from the design and construction of aeroplanes to the making of flight simulators, space satellites and guided weapons.
- **Chemicals**: The chemical industry is the fifth largest in the world, giving jobs to over 250,000 people. Especially the pharmaceutical companies are doing well, and 12 of the world's 50 most popular medicines have been developed in England.
- **Engineering**: British companies have always been among the best machine makers for both the industrial and the transport sector. Today, the country is one of the world's largest producers of tractors.
- **Electronics**: One third of the TV sets in the European Union comes from Britain.
- **Tourism**: The number of tourists from abroad has more than doubled in the last 20 years.

Here are three examples that show some different aspects of 'Working England'.

Farming

England has good land, and 75% of the country-side is used for farming, but only 2% of the English are employed in the farming business, which is not very much in comparison to other European countries. In Denmark and Germany the figure is 4%, and in France 8% of the population make a living from the land.

Cattle.

Farming in England can be divided between crop and cattle farming. Crop farming is mostly found in the eastern and south eastern regions, as this is where most of the lowland is. The most popular crop is wheat, which can be found in nearly half of all the fields, followed by barley, which is grown in a quarter of the farming land.

Cattle farming is found in the country's hilly areas. In fact, England is world famous for several of its cattle breeds. Hereford is probably the beef breed that is known to most people, whereas the Jersey, Guernsey and Ayrshire are known for the high quality milk they produce.

the British Motor Corporation, which became the 3rd largest car company in the world. In 1959 the Morris Mini Minor was put on the market. This car was a masterpiece. It was small, smart and cheap to run, and it has influenced the production of small cars since then.

The name Rolls-Royce has always been connected with an image of exclusiveness and wealth. The famous R's are the initials of the founders: Charles Rolls and Sir Henry Royce. Each car is tailor-made for the customer. The leather for the seats and upholstery inside the cars has always come from Danish cattle as their hides are of such high quality. Not surprisingly, these cars are very expensive to buy.

A Mini.

Rolls-Royce.

Cars

The English are well known for their love of cars, whether this is the everyday Morris Minor or the luxurious Rolls Royce. England's car engineers have always been in sharp competition with each other, and this has made them very creative.

A famous English industrialist who had an enormous influence on the car industry was William Richard Morris. He started out as a bicycle repairman, but 21 years later his first car appeared on the market. It was the Morris-Oxford, an 8.9 horsepower two-seater. This was the beginning of a production of small reliable cars at low prices that revolutionised the industry. After this Morris bought several other car companies, and in 1952 he started

Aston Martin was founded in a small workshop in London in 1914 by Lionel Martin and Robert Bamford. In 90 years the company has only produced 16,000 cars, but 80% of these cars are still in use today. In 1964 the DB5 became world famous appearing in the James Bond film 'Goldfinger'.

Today, many Englishmen are sad to see that their car companies are owned by foreign companies. Rolls-Royce is owned by the German company BMW, Aston Martin and Jaguar are owned by the American cooperation Ford, and Bentley is owned by Volkswagen. The bright side, though, is the fact that several Japanese firms (Toyota, Nissan, Honda) are now producing their cars in Britain.

Fashion

England has always played an important part in the fashion world. One of the first major names was the firm Aquascutum that invented the water-proof Trench coat, which was used in the 1st World War.

In the 1960s Vivienne Westwood hit the headlines with her sexy and eye-catching Punk style, which shocked many people. Believe it or not, the mini skirt was invented in England by Mary Quant. This type of skirt is still popular in fashion today, and no collection is complete without a mini.

Stella McCartney.

Now the clothes scene is full of English trained talents like Stella McCartney and Alexander McQueen. Stella McCartney, the daughter of 'ex-Beatle' Sir Paul McCartney, has worked for several of the big fashion houses, and her designs are worn by many celebrities. McQueen is known as 'Britain's Bad Boy of Fashion', because he is often very rude to the press, but this does not bother his customers, who keep on buying his expensive clothes. Even the 'older' names of fashion are making a comeback, and names like Burberry and Pringle are once again 'hot' and worn by people like Madonna and David Beckham.

Sport and Competition

The Grand National.

Sport and competition play a large role in the lives of most English people. Already in the 19th century, private schools began to teach sport. The schools believed that children should learn about 'fair play', which is not only about keeping the written rules of the game but also keeping the unwritten ones. Pupils were taught that they had to be good losers and that it was the taking part and not the winning that counted. The modern attitude to sport is not quite the same. Nowadays, sport is very professional, and winning is extremely important.

About 29 million people in Britain over the age of 16 regularly take part in some type of sport. However, for many people sport is not only something one does, but also something one watches. England has some special sports events that attract a great number of spectators and TV viewers every year. Here are three examples:

The Grand National is the most popular horse race in England. The track is 7,200 metres long and has 30 jumps of various sizes. The tallest fence is called 'The Chair', which is 155 cm high. Only 40 horses are

The Boat Race.

The Boat Race is one of the more unusual sporting events of the year. 250,000 people line the banks of the River Thames to watch rowing teams from England's oldest universities, Oxford and Cambridge, compete against each other. The race was first rowed in 1829, and from 1845 the course has been rowed from Putney to Mortlake on the River Thames, a distance of 6.8 km. There are eight rowers in each boat, and Cambridge holds the record for the fastest time which is 16 minutes and 19 seconds.

allowed to compete, but because the race is so difficult 40 never finish. In 1984, 23 horses finished, while in 1928 only two finished. Approximately 300 million people around the world watch the race every year.

Wimbledon is the cosy suburb in southwest London, where the famous international Lawn Tennis Championships are held. The first tournament was held in 1877 and was for men only. Women were not allowed to play in the competition until 1884. Wimbledon has always been the favourite championship to win, because it was one of the first important tennis competitions and because of its many traditions. One tradition is that players are asked to play in white or pale coloured clothes. Another tradition is that the spectators eat strawberries and cream between the matches.

A view of the Championships at Wimbledon.

Old Trafford, home of Manchester United.

Today football also means big business. Professional players earn an enormous amount of money, and clubs buy players for their team for even greater amounts. The game is so important now that even politicians become involved in lobbying for the right to hold championships in their area. Some of the most famous English clubs are Manchester United, Liverpool FC, Leeds United and Arsenal FC.

Football

Football is the most popular team sport in the world today. The game started in England in 1863 when the Football Association (FA) was founded and rules were made. Football clubs were created for the working class, and many teams came from local community or church groups. Lots of Englishmen would never dream of kicking a football, but they just love watching the game and being together with other fans. In fact, the English are famous for their fan culture. English fans are completely devoted to the teams they support, even if the teams play bad football. The weekend matches are very important, and English fans follow their teams all over the country. They get together on the stadium terraces waving flags and singing football songs to encourage the players. Many people associate English football with hooligans. In reality, there are only very few English fans that are violent.

Cricket

Bat and ball games were played in England as long ago as the 13th century, and the English speciality cricket probably developed from one of these. It is not a sport that is understood by many, but it is played with great enthusiasm in English-speaking countries (Australia, India, New Zealand, South Africa, Sri Lanka and the West Indies). The game is a bit like baseball. There are two teams with 11 players on each side, and there are two batsmen on the field at a time. They must defend their 'wicket' with their bat and score points by running between the two wickets. A wicket is three wooden poles (called stumps) next to each other with two thin pieces of wood (called the bails) that are balanced on top. If the bails fall, the batter is declared out. The other team 'field', this means that the players try to catch the ball and stop the batters from scoring. There are always two judges, and the matches can take up to five days to play.

One of the most important traditions connected with the game comes from the very first match between England and Australia in 1882. To the horror of England's population, the Australian team beat the English at the famous cricket ground 'The Oval' in London. The press were so shocked that they printed an article suggesting that English cricket was dead and should be burnt. The next year, when the English team was touring Australia, an urn with the ashes of a wicket was given to the English captain. Today, this urn is kept at Lord's Cricket Ground, and Australia and England still play to win the Ashes every second year. Television networks from all over the world spend huge amounts of money to get the rights to broadcast the event, as there are millions of spectators who want to watch it.

Sporting Expressions

Sport is so popular that some sporting expressions are used in everyday language. Here are some examples:

From cricket

On a sticky wicket: a difficult situation

Stumped: unable to answer a question

Have a good innings: have a long life

From boxing

Saved by the bell: saved from a bad situation at the last moment

On the ropes: in a weak position

Throw in the towel: to give up

Win hands down: win easily

From riding

First past the post: the winner

Have the bit between the teeth: determined

In the saddle: in control

From hunting

Run with the pack: to blindly follow others

Go to the dogs: to lead a self-destructive life

freaky facts:

Britain is the only nation that has taken part in every single modern Olympic Games, beginning with the first competition in Athens, Greece, in 1896.

A cricket match at Lord's Cricket Ground.

English Traditions

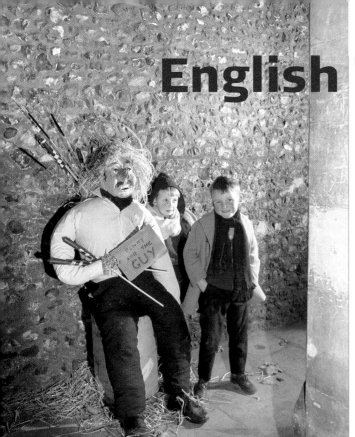

'A penny for the guy.'

Guy Fawkes

Remember, remember the fifth of November,
Gunpowder treason and plot.
We see no reason
Why gunpowder treason
Should ever be forgot.

This is a nursery rhyme that most English children know, and it explains why Guy Fawkes Day is celebrated every year on 5th November. In 1603, after the death of Elizabeth I, James I became the King of England. Like Elizabeth, he was a Protestant, and he made life difficult for all Catholics living in England. By 1605 a small group of Catholics had had enough. They planned to blow up the Houses of Parliament

and kill King James and other Protestant politicians. Somehow word of their plans got out, and Guy Fawkes, one of the conspirators, was caught in the cellars amongst 36 barrels of gunpowder. Both he

Fireworks at Guy Fawkes Night.

and the rest of the group were executed. When the people of London heard that their King had been rescued from a Catholic conspiracy, they started dancing and singing in the streets, and bonfires were lit in triumph. A tradition started that very night, and ever since people have celebrated the occasion with bonfires and fireworks. Nowadays, many children make a 'guy' out of old clothes and newspapers, and they ask people for 'a penny for the guy'. They spend the money on fireworks and the handmade 'guy' ends its days on top of a big bonfire.

Christmas

In England, Christmas is celebrated on 25th December. During December people send Christmas cards to each other. This tradition started many years ago, and the first Christmas card was officially posted in 1840. Today, over a billion Christmas cards pass through the post every year. Many of these cards have idyllic snow-covered landscapes on them, but in fact England very rarely has snow at Christmas time. Traditionally English houses are decorated with holly, ivy and mistletoe. Some follow the custom of 'kissing under the mistletoe', which is a ritual that goes back to the druids (see p. 35 in Religion).

Church services are held at midnight and during the morning on Christmas Day, and afterwards families gather for the big Christmas dinner. The traditional meal consists of stuffed roast turkey, roast potatoes, Brussels sprouts, bread sauce, cranberry jelly, followed by Christmas pudding and brandy butter. The pudding, which consists of dried fruits, butter, nuts and alcohol, is extremely heavy. It is often made weeks in advance and has small

A christmas pudding.

silver charms or coins in it. When it is about to be served, brandy is poured over it and set alight, so it looks like a fireball. Later, when people are just getting their appetites back again, Christmas cake is brought in. This is another heavy fruit cake that is covered by a thick layer of marzipan and icing sugar. After Christmas dinner, people often pull Christmas crackers. These were invented by an English baker in 1846.

*The Palace Pier
in Brighton.*

Summer at the Seaside

Originally, summer holidays only existed for the very rich, as they were the only people who could afford not to work. Towards the end of the 18th century the upper class started a holiday tradition of going to the seaside. This tradition spread to the rest of the population as they began to earn enough money to afford this new luxury.

Among the most popular seaside resorts are the towns of Blackpool on the west coast, Clacton and Southend on the east coast, and Brighton, Eastbourne and Bournemouth on the south coast. Most families stay privately at 'Bed and Breakfasts', where you get your own bedroom and a good English breakfast in the morning. The days are spent swimming and sunbathing. Fun can always be found on the amusement piers. There are bingo halls, discos, playing machines, and lots of cafés and fish and chips shops to keep everybody happy.

freaky facts:

Most holiday resorts sell a special type of sweet: 'rock'. Rock is a hard stick of sugar about 15-20 cm long. It comes in different colours and tastes, and it always has the name of the holiday resort written in it e.g. 'Brighton Rock' or 'Blackpool Rock'.

English Food

The cooking skills of the English have never been as sophisticated as those of the French or the Italian cooks. The English have traditionally been known to eat plenty of meat, fish and chips and sticky puddings.

After many years with a terrible reputation for awful food, things have changed, and the new cuisine of England is hitting the headlines. This time not because it is bad, but because TV cooking has inspired people of all ages to try something different. One of the hottest chefs is the young Jamie Oliver. He has become famous through his series 'The Naked Chef'.

Jamie Oliver.

English Breakfast

Everybody knows that it is important to start the day with a good breakfast. The English take this quite seriously, as you will see if you sit down for a full English breakfast. You will be brought fried eggs and bacon, sausages, fried tomatoes and slices of fried bread, and sometimes also slices of ham and fried potatoes. This is only the first part of the meal, because after all the hot food, slices of fresh toast will be waiting, on which you can put honey, marmalade or Marmite.

freaky facts:

Sandwiches got their name after John Montagu, the Earl of Sandwich. The Earl loved playing cards, but he hated meals, because he had to leave his card games. Finally, he got his servants to serve him meat between slices of bread, which he could eat while he was playing cards. The 'sandwich' was created!

Marmite is an English speciality that is really only eaten by the English. It is a dark brown, sticky and very salty paste that is made from yeast extract. Foreigners usually think that it tastes disgusting, but both children and grown-ups eat it all over England, and it is actually very healthy, because it contains a lot of vitamin B.

All this salty food can make one quite thirsty, so breakfast also includes a big pot of tea. Tea was introduced to England in 1644, and it became so popular that it is now known as the country's traditional drink. Unlike many other Europeans, the English always drink very strong tea with milk and sometimes a bit of sugar as well.

It obviously takes time to prepare such a large breakfast, and nowadays many are very busy in the mornings and do not eat a full breakfast every day. Nowadays, people eat cereals or toast in the morning and only treat themselves to the English breakfast during the weekends.

Fish and Chips

'Fish 'n' chips', as it is pronounced, is England's most famous take-away meal. The meal consists of two ingredients, fish and potatoes, which are simply deep-fried. Added to this, there is the atmosphere of queuing up in your local fish 'n' chip shop listening to the fish sizzling in the oil. The fish is usually cod, and it is covered by a thin batter, which is a kind of dough made of flour, salt and a bit of beer! When both the fish and the chips are ready, they are sprinkled with salt and vinegar and wrapped in a piece of paper to form a cone.

Pub Life

Pubs play a very important role in English social life. The English do not usually invite people around to their private homes unless they are very good friends. Instead many go for an informal drink at their local pub. 'Pub' is short for the official name 'public house', and there are about 50,000 pubs in England.

The atmosphere in a pub is unique. It cannot be compared with anything else. Pubs are supposed to look old, both inside and outside. Even in a new pub, the style must remain old and cosy. The 'oldness' is important, because it brings back memories of the good old days. Pubs often have very small windows, because during the reign of Queen Victoria (1837-1901) drinking was seen to be a bad habit that should not be watched or copied. This is also why very few pubs have tables outside.

Pubs have strict rules concerning children. Alcohol must not be served to anybody under 18, and children under 14 are not even allowed to enter a pub unless food is served there. Pubs do not have waiters, and you have to order your drinks at the bar. This is because many people feel that waiters make things seem more formal, and pubs want their customers to feel as relaxed, as if they were at home.

A pub in Chelsea, London.

freaky facts:

The English invented the world famous 'tomato ketchup'. In France it is called 'English Jam'.

Vocabulary

England – a First Glance

p. 6

impression	Eindruck
bag-lady	obdachlose Frau
pin-striped	nadelgestreift
(to) queue	Schlange stehen
(to) confuse	verwirren
isle	Insel
(to) surround	umgeben
independent	unabhängig
despite	trotz

p. 7

(to) deal with	handeln von

National Symbols

p. 8

patron saint	Schutzheiliger
(to) consist of	bestehen aus
regular	regelmäßig

p. 9

Coat of Arms	Wappen
shield	Schild
(to) support	unterstützen
unicorn	Einhorn
(to) rest upon	ruhen auf
thistle	Distel
shamrock	Kleeblatt
Libya	Libyen
(to) satisfy	zufriedenstellen
(to) offer	anbieten
(to) sacrifice	opfern
Christianity	Christentum
(to) recognise	erkennen

Geography

p. 10

land mark	Wahrzeichen
gorge	Kluft, Schlucht
pleasant	angenehm
range	Bergkette
backbone	Rückgrat
scenery	Landschaft

p. 11

feature	Merkmal
hedge	Hecke
(to) surround	umgeben
wildlife	Tierwelt
quite far north	ziemlich weit nördlich
condition	Bedingung
slight	ein bisschen

p. 12

divide	Grenze
(to) earn a living	seinen Unterhalt verdienen
amount	Menge
(to) provide	sorgen für
(to) contribute	beitragen
(to) extract	herausholen
unemployment	Arbeitslosigkeit
cancer	Krebs
(to) suffer from	leiden an

p. 13

(to) attract	anziehen
(to) cause	hervorrufen, verursachen
(to) expand	steigen
traffic jam	Verkehrsstau
(to) suffer	leiden (unter)
(to) develop	entwickeln
tube	U-Bahn
(to) delay	verspäten
bustle	Hochbetrieb
(to) commute	pendeln
variety	Auswahl, Vielfalt
hardly	kaum
outskirts	Stadtrand

London

p. 14

(to) govern	regieren
passage	Gang
courtyard	Hof
staircase	Treppenhaus
clock face	Zifferblatt

(to) complain	sich beklagen
reign	Regierungszeit
(to) improve	verbessern
Changing of the Guard	Wachablösung

p. 15

medieval	mittelalterlich
fortress	Festung
executioner	Henker
execution	Hinrichtung
experience	Erlebnis
Crown Jewels	Kronjuwelen
(to) guard	bewachen
renowned	berühmt
foggy	neblig
coal heater	Kohlenofen
soot	Ruß
appearance	Aussehen
central heating	Zentralheizung

p. 16

privacy	Privatsphäre
flat	Wohnung
burial	Beerdigung
dome	Kuppel
feature	Attraktion
(to) whisper	flüstern
base	Fundament
exhibition	Ausstellung
ranging from ... to	von ... bis
Chamber of Horrors	Gruselkabinett
Royalty	königliche Personen
(to) found	gründen

p. 17

department store	Warenhaus
grocery store	Lebensmittelgeschäft
department	Abteilung
light bulb	Glühbirne
bird's eye view	Vogelperspektive

England Under Attack

p. 18

invading force	einmarschierende Macht
AD (Anno Domini)	nach Christi Geburt
(to) occupy	besetzen
(to) force upon	aufzwingen
major	besonders große
outpost	Außenposten
(to) originate	zurückgehen auf
(to) overrun	überlaufen
knight	Ritter
(to) be tempted	in Versuchung geführt werden
wealth	Reichtum
(to) raid	plündern
monastery	Kloster
(to) conquer	erobern, besiegen
(to) settle	sich niederlassen
(to) challenge	herausfordern
(to) divide	aufteilen
Danelaw	Danelagen, Gebiet des dänischen Rechts in England

p. 19

duke	Herzog
(to) defeat	besiegen
(to) reward	belohnen
nobleman	Edelmann
peasant	Lehensbauer
branch	Linie, Zweig
in disguise	verkleidet
resistance	Widerstand
deep in thought	in tiefen Gedanken
(to) accuse	anklagen
(to) tell off	einen Rüffel geben

Two Great Rulers: Henry VIII and Elizabeth I

p. 20

ruler	Herrscher
(to) unite	vereinigen
(to) pass on	weitergeben, weitervererben
(to) found	gründen

(to) behead	enthaupten
(to) execute	hinrichten
traitor	Verräter

p. 21

Virgin Queen	die jungfräuliche Königin
reign	Regierungszeit
galleon	Galeone (großes Kriegs- und Handelsschiff)
(to) bless	segnen
(to) sneeze	niesen
plague	Pest

The Industrial Revolution

p. 22

extensive	umfassend
manual work	Arbeit – mit Handkraft ausgeführt
knowledge	Wissen
steam	Dampf
manufacture	Herstellung
goods	Waren
textile	Textil, Stoff
agricultural revolution	landwirtschaftliche Revolution

p. 23

(to) employ	anstellen
labour	Arbeitskraft
foreman	Vorarbeiter
condition	Bedingung
(to) publish	veröffentlichen
thigh	Oberschenkel
(to) whip	peitschen
gradual	allmählich
compulsory	obligatorisch
(to) reduce	reduzieren, verringern
death rate	Todesrate

From Empire to Commonwealth

p. 24

empire	Imperium
Commonwealth	Commonwealth
(to) encourage	fördern
exploration	Erforschung
trading company	Handelsgesellschaft
newly	kürzlich

(to) discover	entdecken

p. 25

throughout	durch ... hindurch
(to) gain	erlangen
treaty	Vertrag
(to) allow	erlauben
(to) set	untergehen
spice	Gewürz
nutmeg	Muskatnuss
cotton	Baumwolle
indigo	Indigo (tief dunkelblauer Farbstoff)
item	Ding
incident	Vorfall
(to) capture	gefangen nehmen
suffocation	Erstickung
(to) gather	sammeln
(to) seize	beschlagnahmen
conquest	Eroberung
(to) remain	übrig bleiben
the Dutch	Holländer
(to) last	dauern
(to) take possession	einnehmen
(to) settle	sich niederlassen
orphan	Waisenkind
pickpocket	Taschendieb
(to) range from	sich zwischen ... und ... bewegen
theft	Diebstahl
pond	Teich
practice	Praxis

p. 26

goods	Waren
(to) take possession	in Besitz nehmen
independent	unabhängig
former	ehemalig
(to) co-operate	kooperieren, zusammenarbeiten
(to) gain	erlangen
(to) suspend	ausschließen
human rights	Menschenrechte

The World Wars

p. 27

(to) be sup-posed to be	sein sollen
(to) encourage	auffordern
(to) appeal	appellieren
sense of duty	Pflichtgefühl
(to) volunteer	sich freiwillig melden
trench	Schützengraben
casualties	Verluste

p. 28

death toll	Gesamtzahl der Toten
(to) suffer	leiden
shell shock	Kriegstrauma
mental break-down	Nervenzusam-menbruch
society	Gesellschaft
(to) gain	bekommen, erlangen
(to) be allowed to	dürfen
peace treaty	Friedensvertrag
uneasy	unangenehm
calm	Ruhe
(to) settle	sich senken
(to) vanish	verschwinden

p. 29

stage	Etappe
coastal	Küsten-
airfield	Flugplatz
airforce	Luftwaffe
(to) carry out	durchführen
raid	Angriff
(to) realise	erkennen, ein-sehen
(to) remain	zurückbleiben
air raid shelter	Luftschutzraum
(to) be in short supply	knapp sein
petrol	Benzin
(to) surround	umgeben
(to) ally	sich verbünden
(to) commit suicide	Selbstmord begehen
gradually	allmählich

The British Parliament

p. 30

authority	Autorität, Gewalt
(to) consist of	bestehen aus
House of Commons	Unterhaus
House of Lords	Oberhaus
general elec-tions	Parlaments-wahl(en)
constituency	Wahlkreis
(to) form	bilden
issue	(Streit)frage, Thema
(to) fix	fixieren, fest-legen
judge	Richter
hereditary peer	Peer, Edelmann, der seinen Titel geerbt hat
(to) inherit	erben
life peer	Mitglied des Oberhauses, dessen Titel nicht weiterver-erbt wird

p. 31

(to) honour	ehren
(to) refer to	sich beziehen auf
unity	Einheit
advice	Rat(schlag)
competition	Wettkampf
(to) nickname	den Spitznamen geben
wealthy	wohlhabend
well-being	Wohl
shape	Form
debating room	ungefähr: Ple-narsaal
(to) fit	passen zu
minority	Minderheit

p. 32

the Speaker	Vorsitzender des Unter-hauses
chairman	Diskussions-leiter
(to) expect	erwarten
(to) take part	teilnehmen
neither ... nor	weder ... noch
(to) prepare	vorbereiten
(to) interrupt	unterbrechen
rude	unhöflich
(to) object to	Einspruch er-heben
coward	Feigling
traitor	Verräter
(to) banish	ausweisen

The Monarchy

p. 33

monarchy	Monarchie
supreme head	Oberhaupt
(to) remove	entfernen
public	Öffentlichkeit

p. 34

(to) associate	verbinden
horse-drawn carriage	Kutsche
tax-payer	Steuerzahler
break-up	Trennung
charitable	wohltätig
admiration	Bewunderung
funeral	Beerdigung
(to) regain	wiedergewin-nen
occasion	Gelegenheit
conman	Betrüger

Religion

p. 35

responsible	verantwortlich
solstice	Sonnenwende
(to) worship	anbeten
feast days	Festtage
(to) gather	sammeln
mistletoe	Mistel(zweig)
oak tree	Eiche
(to) please	jdn. zufrieden stellen

p. 36

on a regular basis	regelmäßig
community	Gemeinschaft
Pope	Papst
strong-willed	willensstark
(to) apply	ansuchen um
(to) refuse	ablehnen
determined	entschlossen
male heir	männlicher Erbe
Defender of the Faith	Verteidiger des Glaubens
reformer	Reformator
(to) want one's own way	seinen Willen durchsetzen wollen
(to) be fond of	mögen

p. 37

(to) appoint	ernennen
dean	Dompropst, Superinten-dent

Salvation Army	die Heilsarmee
Pentecostal Churces	die Pfingstbewegung
trader	Händler
majority	Mehrheit
mosque	Moschee
(to) worship	anbeten
(to) settle	sich niederlassen
conquest	Eroberung
ancestor	Vorfahr
(to) flee	flüchten
persecution	Verfolgung

The English

p. 38

(to) fix	festlegen, fixieren
bobby	Polizist
(to) consider	sich betrachten als
apparent	offenbar
reign	Regierungszeit
(to) declare	erklären
long since	schon längst
razor sharp	messerscharf
wit	Verstand, Witz
countless	unzählig
pearl button	Perlenknopf
(to) sew	nähen
average	durchschnittlich
(to) rhyme	sich reimen

p. 39

strife	Streit
society	Gesellschaft
(to) flee	flüchten
oppression	Unterdrückung
(to) escape	entfliehen
port	Hafen
serial killer	Serienmörder

p. 40

refugee	Flüchtling
(to) encourage	ermutigen
(to) rebuild	wiederaufbauen
recently	kürzlich
(to) be reflected in	sich widerspiegeln in
reindeer antler	Rentiergeweih
(to) pull the funniest faces	die lustigsten Gesichter schneiden
master of ceremonies	Zeremonienmeister
steep	steil

rough	hart, grob

p. 41

(to) let off	abbrennen
fireworks	Feuerwerk
ancient	(ur)alt

Schools

p. 42

(to) receive	erhalten
(to) remain	übrig bleiben
school fee	Schulgeld
average	durchschnittlich
primary school	Grundschule bis zur ca. 6. Klasse
government-funded	staatlich unterstützt
(to) establish	etablieren, gründen
(to) spread	verbreiten
value	Wert
honesty	Ehrlichkeit
integrity	Integrität
team spirit	Gemeinschaftsgeist, Zusammenhalt
(to) realise	einsehen
available	zugänglich, erreichbar
local council	Stadtrat
(to) encourage	ermutigen

p. 43

(to) provide	sorgen für
subject	Fach
monk's cassock	Mönchskutte
label	Marke
(to) tease	hänseln
brand	Marke
(to) deal with	umgehen mit
probable	wahrscheinlich
boarding school	Internat
(to) equip	ausstatten
(to) employ	anstellen

p. 44

former	ehemalig
legal world	die juristische Welt
percent	Prozent
half terms	Herbst- und Winterferien

p. 45

unit	Einheit
spare time	Freizeit
(to) found	gründen
(to) attract	anziehen
degree	akademischer Grad
(to) affect	beeinflussen
refectory	Speisesaal
(to) say grace	das Tischgebet sprechen
annual	jährlich
(to) nickname	den Spitznamen geben
'red-brick'	roter Backstein
satchel	Schultasche

Working England

p. 46

trading nation	Handelsnation
aerospace	Luftfahrt
(to) handle	sich befassen mit, sich beschäftigen mit
guided weapon	Fernlenkwaffe
pharmaceutical	pharmazeutisch
engineering	Technik
abroad	Ausland
farming	Landwirtschaft
in comparison	verglichen mit

p. 47

crop	Ernte
cattle	Vieh
wheat	Weizen
barley	Gerste
breed	Züchtung

p. 48

influence	Einfluss
(to) appear	erscheinen
two-seater	Zwei-Sitzer
reliable	zuverlässig
wealth	Reichtum
founder	Gründer
tailor-made	maßgeschneidert
upholstery	Polster
hide	Haut

p. 49

(to) found	gründen
(to) appear	auftreten

foreign	ausländisch, Auslands-
waterproof	wasserdicht
Trench coat	Trenchcoat
(to) hit the headlines	Schlagzeilen machen
eye-catching	Aufmerksamkeit erregend
collection	Modekollektion
complete	vollständig
rude	unhöflich
(to) bother	stören

Sport and Competition

p. 50

attitude	Haltung, Einstellung
quite	ganz
event	Ereignis
track	Rennstrecke
various	verschieden
fence	Hindernis

p. 51

(to) be allowed to	dürfen
(to) compete	konkurrieren
bank	Ufer
course	Strecke
cosy	gemütlich
suburb	Vorort
lawn	Rasen
pale	hell, blass
cream	Sahne

p. 52

(to) found	gründen
community	Gemeinde
devoted to	hingebungsvoll
terrace	Rang
(to) encourage	ermuntern
(to) associate	verbinden
batsman	Schlagmann
field	Spielfeld
(to) defend	verteidigen
wicket	Tor
pole	Pfahl
stump	Querholz
bail	Latte
(to) declare	erklären
(to) field	im Feld sein

p. 53

horror	Entsetzen
(to) suggest	andeuten
(to) broadcast	senden
expression	Ausdruck
innings	Halbzeit (in Kricket)
bit	Gebiss
determined	entschlossen
pack	Meute

English Traditions

p. 54

gunpowder	Schießpulver
treason	Landesverrat
plot	Verschwörung
nursery rhyme	Kinderreim
(to) blow up	in die Luft sprengen
(to) get out	sich herumsprechen
conspirator	Verschwörer
cellar	Keller
barrel	Fass

p. 55

(to) execute	hinrichten
(to) rescue	retten
conspiracy	Verschwörung
bonfire	Freudenfeuer
occasion	Ereignis
fireworks	Feuerwerk
rarely	selten
holly	Stechpalme
ivy	Efeu
mistletoe	Mistel(zweig)
custom	Brauch
church service	Gottesdienst
(to) stuff	ausstopfen, füllen
roast turkey	Putenbraten
Brussel sprouts	Rosenkohl
bread sauce	weiße Soße mit Paniermehl, Zwiebeln und Gewürzen
cranberry	Preiselbeere
pudding	Pudding, Nachspeise
brandy butter	Cognacbutter
in advance	im Voraus
charm	Talisman

(to) set alight	anzünden
icing sugar	Puderzucker, Zuckerguss
cracker	Knallbonbon

p. 56

seaside resort	Badeort
amusement pier	Pier mit verschiedenen Vergnügen

English Food

p. 57

skill	Fähigkeit
sticky	klebrig
pudding	Nachtisch
cuisine	Küche, Kochkunst
(to) hit the headlines	Schlagzeilen machen
fried egg	Spiegelei
ham	Schinken

p. 58

paste	Paste
yeast	Hefe
(to) contain	enthalten
obvious	deutlich
cereals	Cornflakes u.a.
(to) treat oneself to	sich selbst verwöhnen mit
(to) pronounce	aussprechen
(to) deep-fry	fritieren
(to) queue up	Schlange stehen
(to) sizzle	brutzeln
cod	Dorsch
batter	Rührteig
dough	Teig
(to) sprinkle	bestreuen
vinegar	Essig
(to) wrap	einpacken
cone	Kegel

p. 59

cosy	gemütlich
reign	Regierungszeit
habit	Gewohnheit
concerning	was ... betrifft
(to) be allowed to	dürfen
relaxed	entspannt